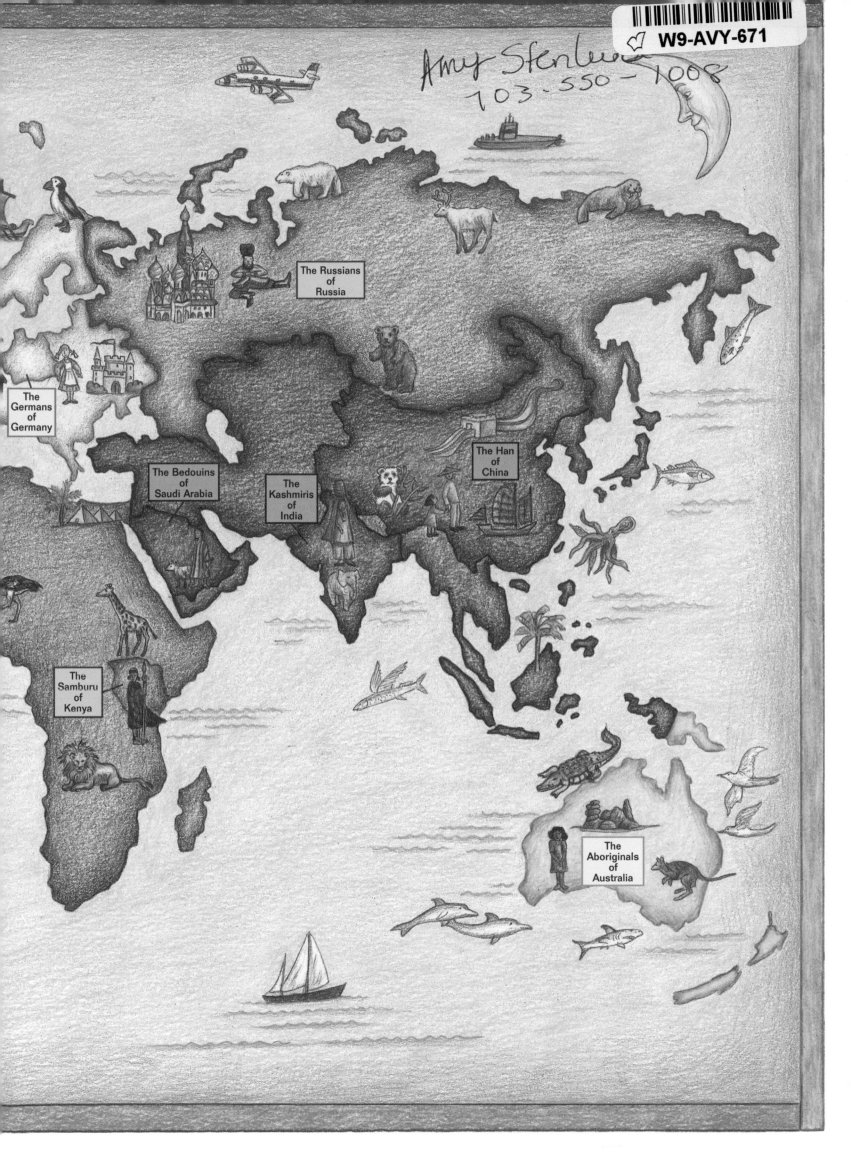

All the Children
OF THE WORLD

by

Karen Mezek Leimert

WORD PUBLISHING
Dallas·London·Vancouver·Melbourne

For Walter, solid as a rock,
For Katya, happy as a lark,
For Harry, chattery as a chimp,
For Max, bouncy as a ball,
And for Estella, thanks for helping us all!

ALL THE CHILDREN OF THE WORLD

Text and illustrations copyright © 1996 by Karen Mezek Leimert.

Scripture quotations used in this book are from the *International Children's Bible*,
copyright © 1987, 1988 by Word Publishing, Dallas, TX 75234.

All artwork was created on Strathmore Bristol paper with Prismacolor pencil.

The adaptation of Reverend C. H. Woolston's "Jesus Loves the Little Children"
is from #75 of the SEE and KNOW series by Mrs. Dan Whitaker.
Published and copyrighted by Sentinel Publishing Co., 1980. Used by permission.

Managing Editor: Laura Minchew
Project Editor: Beverly Phillips

Library of Congress Cataloging-in-Publication Data

Leimert, Karen Mezek, 1956–
  All the children of the world / by Karen Mezek Leimert ; illustrated by Karen Mezek Leimert
    p. cm.
  "Word kids!"
  Summary: Celebrates different cultures around the world, from Iowa to Portugal.
  ISBN 0–8499–1310–1 (secular)
  ISBN 0–8499–1309–8 (Christian)
  1. Children—Cross-cultural studies—Juvenile literature. 2. Manners and customs—Juvenile literature.
[1. Manners and customs.]   I. Title.
  GN482.L45   1996
  305.23—dc20   95–48811
                                                                                     CIP
                                                                                      AC

Printed in Mexico

96 97 98 99 00 RRD 9 8 7 6 5 4 3 2 1

CONTENTS

Jesus Loves the Little Children

INTRODUCTION

The children of the world live in nations with borders. Nations come and go and borders change, but people remain the same, enduring hardships, enjoying times of plenty, and raising their children as best they can no matter what the circumstances. Each nation may have its own customs and traditions, but in this one way we are all united: In our love for our children, we stand together in a common hope and prayer. May God give us the courage and wisdom to raise our children to follow His path.

For God loved the world so much that he gave his only Son. God gave his Son so that whoever believes in him may not be lost, but have eternal life.

—John 3:16

The Amazonians
OF BRAZIL

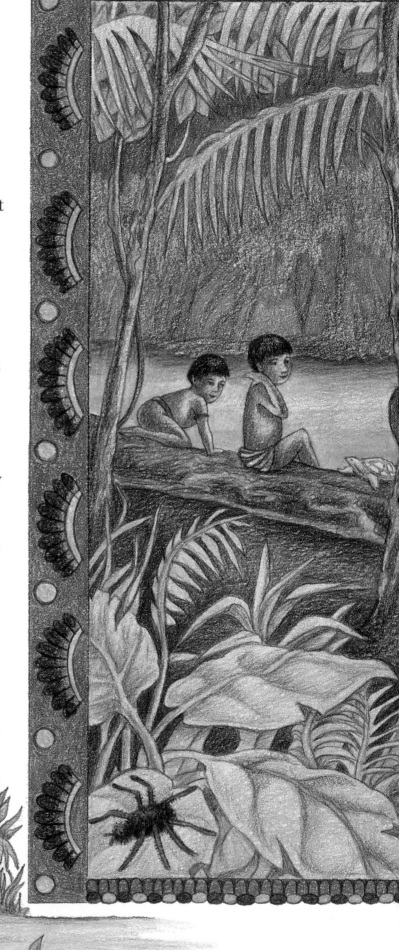

The Amazon rain forest is a wild place, still mainly unexplored and filled with mysteries. Flowing through it is a river so deep and wide that one of its islands is as large as the country of Switzerland. The towering trees grow with amazing speed and are bursting with life. Parrots squawk, and monkeys chatter and howl. Insects scurry along the jungle floor, buzzing, humming, scratching, scraping.

The many tribes of the Amazon are perfectly at home in the forest. They can travel for miles through a tangled maze of branches and vines, never losing their way and never tiring. Their children play in the river, sharing it with the pink dolphin, the razor-toothed piranha, and the deadly anaconda snake.

Over time, the Amazonians have gathered a wealth of knowledge about the plants and animals around them. They have learned how to hunt and fish, grow vegetables, and gather wild fruits in special ways that allow the land to renew itself.

A steady flow of settlers has come to the rain forest, hoping for a better life. Miners dig for riches, and scientists search for medical cures. The Amazon has much to offer, but it is a delicately balanced wonderland. Care and respect are the keys to its survival.

Jesus loves . . .

The Kashmiris
OF INDIA

At the foot of the Himalayas lies legendary Kashmir. Long ago, kings, princes, and merchants passed through this valley of emerald green, following the trading routes from India to China.

Travelers still come from far and wide to see the beauty of Kashmir. They walk through lush gardens filled with flowers. They glide along lavender blue lakes in small beautifully painted boats called *shikaras*.

The hard-working Kashmiris have no time for such luxuries. They work from daybreak to day's end, planting rice in the fields and harvesting the fruit-laden trees. Young children sell bright pink lotus blossoms to the visitors. But they keep the giant lotus leaves for animal food.

With the coming of autumn, the trees turn orange and brown, and the travelers disappear. When the clouds bring ice and snow, the Kashmiris keep themselves warm by carrying hot coals in special wicker baskets beneath their cloaks.

The villagers do not rest during the winter. They are masters of many arts. Some weave carpets and shawls like those once treasured by the wealthy maharajah rulers of old. From generation to generation, these talents have been faithfully passed down from parents to children until the present time.

the little children . . .

The Bedouins
of Saudi Arabia

In the deserts of Saudi Arabia the dunes stand as high as tall buildings, and the flat rocks shimmer in the scorching sun. Sudden winds whip the sand into clouds of yellowish darkness. Dust and small stones fly through the air like red-hot darts.

This is the land of the Bedouin nomads. They wander the trackless desert, pitching their tents wherever there is water and grass for their herds. They live on dates, rice, and the milk of their camels, loving the ill-tempered animals like children.

Despite their hard life, the Bedouins are among the friendliest of people. A stranger arriving in their camp is welcomed with open arms. If necessary, the guest is defended against enemies, and for three days he is cared for, even if it means the Bedouins go hungry.

In the evenings children play beyond the tents, watching for the Suhail star. They know that when it rises in the southern sky, the autumn rains will follow. With the first cloudburst, green shoots of grass appear, signaling the end of summer and the welcome relief of cooler days. For the rains as well as the sandstorms, for the winds and the grass, for all things good and bad, the Bedouins give thanks.

all the children . . .

The Maya
OF MEXICO

Long before the Spanish explorers arrived in Mexico searching for gold and riches, the Mayan people had built for themselves an advanced culture. In huge cities of stone, they studied science, made precise calendars, and added the concept of zero to mathematics.

Today these great cities are gone. No one knows why this great civilization lost its glory, but Mayan Indians still live in the Yucatan Peninsula.

In the early morning, women carry bowls of corn kernels to the village tortilla shop to be ground into flour. Draped around their shoulders are colorful *rebozo* shawls, hand-woven from wool. Babies are carried snugly in the *rebozos,* their dark heads peeking out from the folds of soft cloth.

On market days the Indians sell sweet oranges, limes and papayas, or red-hot chili peppers in the town square. Bananas are piled high, some as tiny as a finger and others as big as a shoebox. Children run between the stacks of fruit and vegetables, laughing and shouting.

When evening comes, the families return to their *palapa* huts of wood and straw. In swinging hammocks, the children are gently rocked to sleep as a soft breeze caresses their faces.

of the world.

The Inuit
OF CANADA

Far to the north, in a land of ice and bitter cold, live the people known as Eskimos. The term is not a nice one, for it means "those who eat raw meat." Before they were called Eskimos, one group named themselves *the Inuit,* which simply means "the people."

Many might imagine the polar world to be lonely, desolate, and dangerous, but these are words that could also be used to describe a big, bustling city. The Inuit have adapted amazingly well to this harsh environment. They have learned to build their igloos round, for if they built them square, the storm-driven snow crystals would slice the edges off and leave great gaping holes. Mothers carry their babies close to their bodies to keep them warm. Then they wrap themselves in thick sealskin coats.

Except briefly in July, the temperature does not rise above freezing. For months at a time, all they see is night, and it is hard to tell where the ground ends and the water begins.

Even so, the Inuit do not find their land depressing. In fact, many of them call it "the beautiful land." Explorers of old marveled that the Inuit believed themselves to be the happiest people on earth.

Any color . . .

The Aboriginals
OF AUSTRALIA

Australia is the world's largest island and also its smallest continent. For many centuries this land of contrasts has been the home of the Aboriginals, or "native people."

Along the northern riverbanks of the country, a tropical paradise grows, filled with paperbark, mangrove, and rivergum trees. Farther inland lies the flattest, driest region on earth, the Australian Outback.

To survive in this burning desert, Aboriginal children must learn to read the land as others might read a book. They know that the baobab tree holds pockets of precious water in its trunk. They have learned that a handful of desert insect larvae makes a healthy meal. And they know a delicious nectar can be drunk from the swollen sacks on the backs of the honey ants.

These ancient people never built a temple or a pyramid. They never developed a wheel, made pottery, or wove cloth. They have no written language and no permanent dwellings. To them, the land cannot be bought or sold. It cannot be owned, and it should not be changed. The Aboriginals have no desire to make the land into something other than what it is, for they believe it is already perfect in every way.

dark . . .

The Germans
OF GERMANY

The nation of Germany is a little more than a hundred years old, yet Germanic tribes have lived in this land for many centuries. These mighty warriors fought fiercely for their families and homeland, crushing the powerful armies of the Roman Empire.

On craggy peaks, in forests and beside rivers, the ruined castles of bandits and barons stand as reminders of the legendary knights and maidens of old. The Germans have always been master storytellers. In wide-eyed wonder, children listen to tales of Tom Thumb, Little Red Riding Hood, and Hansel and Gretel. The Brothers Grimm traveled the countryside, collecting these fables from the common folk and writing them down in thick volumes for others to enjoy.

In the Black Forest, villagers carve cuckoo clocks from the wood of fir trees. In the old days every household in the village worked together, each one carefully making a delicate piece. On and on each little clock would travel, from one family to the next, until at last it reached the final house where all the parts were fitted together. In this time-honored way, the people of Germany could turn a simple clock into a beautiful work of art.

or light . . .

The Iowans
OF THE UNITED STATES

On the plains of Iowa the grass grows as tall as a man, stretching on and on forever as far as the eyes can see. It wasn't long ago that bison roamed these plains, feeding on the sweet meadows and drinking from the clear rivers. But no matter how much they ate or drank, there was always plenty more.

Iowa's first settlers were mostly native-born Americans whose ancestors had come from every corner of the earth. These settlers found a wide-open land of opportunity. Across this rich black earth they built their farms and towns, creating the look of a colorful patchwork quilt on the prairie.

A farmer's life is ruled by the weather and by the changing seasons. He sees and understands the beauty in the perfectly straight lines of a well-plowed field. His children play among waving stalks of yellow corn. And on lazy afternoons they sit by streams with hook and line, waiting for the fish to bite. At dusk they run through shadowy woods, chasing fireflies that twinkle among the trees like stars fallen from heaven.

On Sundays the farmers rest their plows and bring their families to white-steepled churches. There they pray to God and thank Him for the richness of their land and life.

they are . . .

The Samburu
OF KENYA

On the dry, lowlands of eastern Africa live one of the last remaining warrior tribes, the Samburu. When the young boys become warriors, they move away from their families and live out in the open, hunting buffalo and antelope and other game. At night they sleep beneath the stars, listening for the low growl of lions.

The Samburu respect and care for each member of their group, from the oldest grandmother to the youngest child. The families awaken before dawn, rising when the early morning star appears in the still-dark sky. Women milk the cows, singing softly to calm them. Then the animals are led out to graze. Children are taught from an early age to tend the herds. The elders of the tribe make sure that each precious animal is closely watched to keep it safe from hungry lions and cheetahs. With the setting of the sun, the herds are brought back home again.

Many Samburu now go to the city to study and to work. Yet they are often drawn back to the wild beauty of their homeland. Here, beneath Mount Lololokwi, the Samburu watch over one another, safe and secure in their traditional family ways.

precious . . .

The Samoans
OF UPOLU, WESTERN SAMOA

The island of Upolu is surrounded by white sandy beaches and waters of aqua blue. Rumbling volcanic mountains sometimes spit out lava high into the sky. Steep ridges are thick with palms, ferns, and creeping vines. Waterfalls tumble down mossy cliffs into clear, deep pools.

Many people have come to Samoa searching for paradise. Pirates once sailed these seas, attacking ships and burying their treasures in secret hideaways on Upolu and the surrounding islands. Poets and painters followed, drawing inspiration from the beauty of the people and their land. But to the Samoans, this has always simply been their home, providing them with all their modest needs.

A Samoan *fale,* or house, has no walls, windows, or doors, only a thatched coconut-leaf roof supported by poles. The family sleeps on mats on a floor of coral. Early in the morning the sun awakens them, peeking through the coconut-leaf blinds that hang from the roof.

Each day children bring flowers to decorate their school. Flowers grow everywhere on Upolu, and their brilliance is more prized than jewels. Shining in the dark hair of a Samoan child, a halo of pink and red hibiscus blooms looks lovelier than a ruby-studded crown.

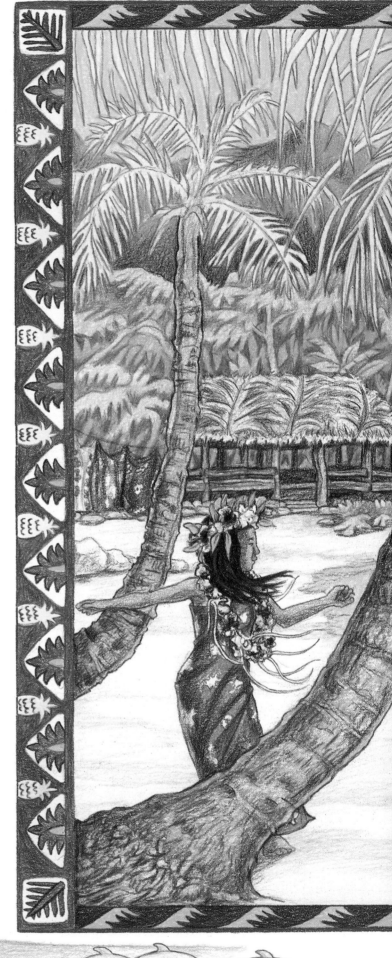

in His sight.

The Russians
OF RUSSIA

On the marshy flatlands of northwestern Russia, Peter the Great built the majestic city of St. Petersburg. Its enchanting beauty inspired many of the world's greatest works of art, poetry, and literature. The treasure houses of the czars were filled with gold, and their crowns were covered in diamonds and rubies, emeralds and sapphires.

St. Petersburg has never lost its beauty, but the real treasure of Russia lies in the timeless forests and fields of the countryside. Here the people have kept the old Russian ways alive in song and dance and in their faith in God. This faith is so strong, so deep, that the word for peasant, *Krestyanin,* simply means "a Christian." In the villages they greet each other not by name, but as Mother or Father, Brother or Sister.

Most village houses have a bench outside where families sit on summer evenings. After a simple meal, often of cabbage soup and black bread, older family members love to sing and tell the children ancient folk tales, like "The Firebird." These stories speak of the mighty Russian spirit—the victory of the humble over the powerful and of the courage of a true and pure heart.

Jesus loves . . .

The Han
OF CHINA

In northern China, along the banks of the Yellow River, the Han built one of the greatest empires history has ever known. Emperor after emperor rose and fell, building splendid cities that shone for a time, then crumbled.

One out of every five people in the world is Chinese. Most Chinese are of Han ancestry, and they are spread across their land like the waters of the sea. The Han see themselves as one great family, rooted to the same soil, breathing the same air, and working together for the common good.

Mostly they are farmers, living in small villages, each one within walking distance of the next. Their houses are made of mud or brick with roofs of thatched straw. In muddy rice fields, they work all day, untying the young green shoots and carefully planting them in tidy rows.

In village schools children begin the long task of learning to read and write Chinese. There are not tens, or hundreds, but *thousands* of characters to be memorized, each one a little different from the next. Calligraphy, the ability to paint these characters with beauty and grace, is considered by the Han to be the highest of all art forms. With just the right swish of a brush, a masterpiece can be created from a simple Chinese letter.

the little children . . .

The Portuguese
OF PORTUGAL

At the tip of Algarve, Portugal, a lighthouse stands looking out to sea. In olden times this jutting piece of land was thought to be the end of the world. Greeks and Romans who visited these shores told stories of a sun that hissed as it sank beneath the waves of the far-off horizon. To medieval sailors this was the Sea of Darkness, where the waters boiled, turned thick like jelly, or plunged off the earth into nothingness.

Such tales did not stop the Portuguese from exploring beyond the "end of the earth." They built sea-going galleons as finely crafted as a modern spaceship, and their courage was no different from that of an astronaut blasting off into outer space.

The sea has now been mastered, and the stories have been turned into legends, but the Portuguese still love their ocean. On dark winter evenings, fishermen track fat tuna and sardines that swim just off the shore. Night after night they chase the fish, throwing their nets to catch the silvery creatures.

With the coming of dawn, the fishermen point their boats homeward. Sparkling in the rising sun, the waves turn fiery pink and gold. The children run to the shore and gaze across the sea, reaching out as if to touch the other side.

of the world.

JESUS LOVES THE LITTLE CHILDREN

Jesus loves the little children,
All the children of the world.
Any color, dark or light,
They are precious in His sight.
Jesus loves the little children of the world.

—Adapted by Mrs. Dan Whitaker

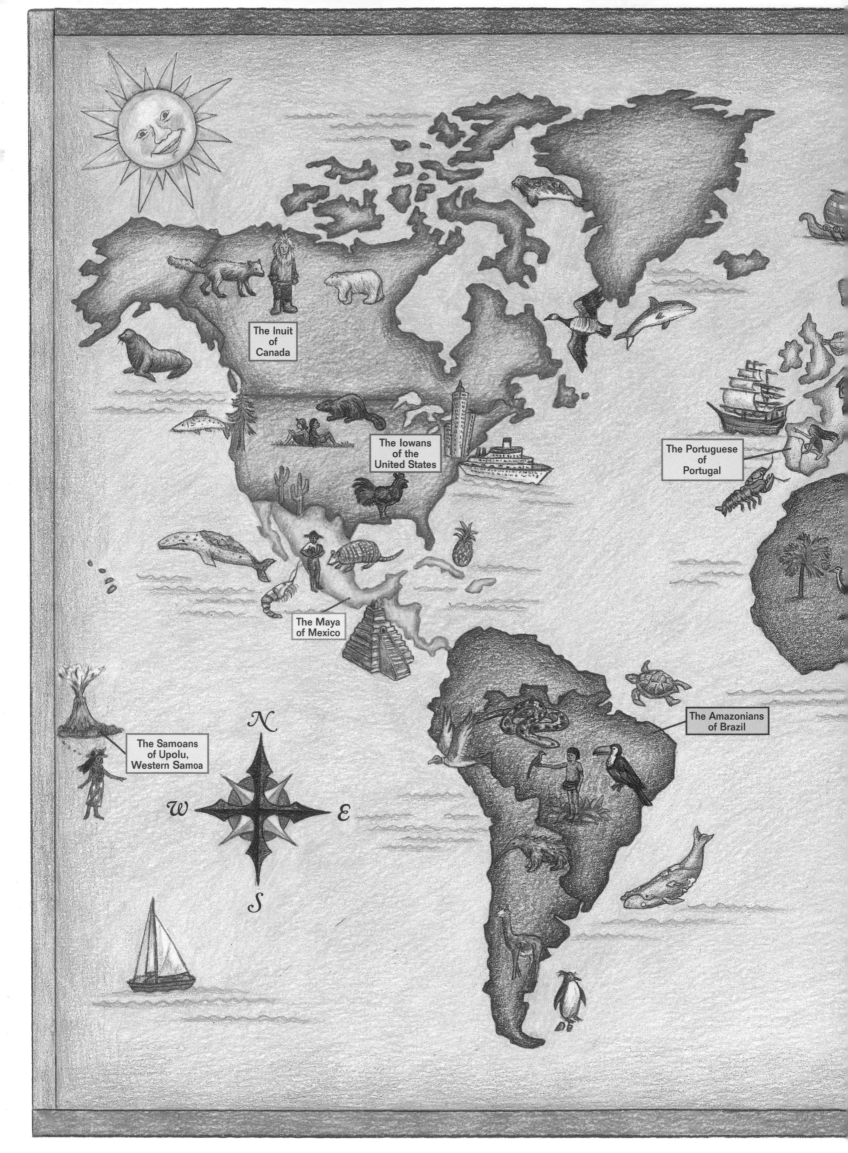

The Inuit
of
Canada

The Iowans
of the
United States

The Portuguese
of
Portugal

The Maya
of Mexico

The Amazonians
of Brazil

The Samoans
of Upolu,
Western Samoa

N

W

E

S